Songs of My Spirit

Peggy McCardle

PublishAmerica
Baltimore

First printing

ISBN: 1-4137-0858-7
PUBLISHED BY PUBLISHAMERICA, LLLP
www.publishamerica.com
Baltimore

Printed in the United States of America

Dedication

This book is dedicated to my parents, Guy and Irene McCardle, two wonderful, thoughtful, kind and hardworking people who taught me to appreciate life, to see the colors and hear the music, and to love. I love you, Mom and Dad.

Acknowledgement

I wish to acknowledge my family, who always believed I could be a writer, even when I did not; my husband, Robert Martschinske, who continues to inspire and support my poetry, and who said it was what made him fall in love with me; and my friend and fiction co-author, Brian Hartford, who never fails to encourage me. There are many, many others who are there for me on a daily basis. If I tried to acknowledge all the wonderful people in my life who have inspired and encouraged my writing, especially my poetry, I would surely omit some. You all know who you are. Thank you, with all my heart.

List of Poems

Songs of My Spirit

Dusk

leaves fade
the paint on the fence
becomes a lifeless shade
and consciousness is suspended
between sun and total darkness

Midnight

in crisp cool green
dew damp fingers of fern
unfurling
beckon me to ruby dreams

a tree of towering
midnight green
is silhouetted darkly
against a blue-black rain sky

in dim light
shadows grow grotesque
only shadows of the mind
less fearsome than reality
yet more acute

in light years
a single ray
explodes one ruby dream

Du Temps Perdus

The tastes of warm affection,
macaroons and tea,
my Proustian madeleine
on a chilly autumn Saturday
evoke sensations long past,
of Grandma's house,
fresh macacroons from the oven,
the scent tempered with whiffs
of used tobacco
and Pap-pap's pipe, unlighted,
pulling his smile to one side.
After he'd gone
the pipes stood at attention
in a solemn circle
on the stand in the bathroom.
Somehow the cookies and tea
weren't quite the same after that.
Tell me, Marcel,
where do I go now
a la recherche
du temps perdus?

Clear-eyed Innocent

I am a child on a carousel horse
riding on wings of faith
Call me Pegasus
I am free

The Icy Silver Sun

The icy silver sun in the winter trees
climbs toward daylight,
Reveals a group of birds
As they lift in unison.
They move in concert
to a tall barren tree
Unhesitatingly, they find their places,
a black-clad orchestra,
like notes returning to sheet music,
writing a melody
on the cold winter sky.

Happy Trails to You

My favorite childhood game
was Cowboys and Indians.
No one ever wanted to be an Indian --
they all got killed.
In fact, sometimes the game
was just called Cowboys.
Free of the harassment
of our misunderstood indigenes,
I always wanted to be Roy Rogers
Or, failing that,
his faithful dog Bullet.
Even Trigger, his horse
sometimes got to save the day.
When the boys played
they tried to relegate me
to the role of Dale Evans,
who rode a horse called Buttermilk
and got to come along.
But I didn't restrict myself
to female roles, then.
Roy was my role model.
I had a little golden record
of his songs;
Dale sang along.
So did I.
Am I still singing along?
And when will we meet again, Roy?

Epidemic

On foggy days of adolescence,
I used to wander
through streets and woods
alone with my thoughts,
at peace, or seeking
and usually finding it,
listening to the sounds
of sneakers on wet pavement,
enjoying the anonymity of the mist.

Today...
the long solitary walk in the rain
didn't really help,
but the fine mist clouded my glasses
so no one could tell that tears
clouded my sight
when happy children ran inside
to warm dry kitchens with food smells.
The little boy with AIDS died today.
He had no one
to call him in out of the rain
or cook him chili and hot dogs
or walk him to the school bus
because mommy had already died
and daddy was gone, maybe dead too.

Why didn't a long solitary walk in the rain
make me feel better?
The sadness will pass
but I know it will return
again and again
because the little boy with AIDS
who died today
is not the only one.

Sunset

In a sky
delicate china blue
with cobalt purpling clouds,
a gossamer sun
kneels
and dies.

A dusk disappearing cloud
caught craggy
in a dead tree,
stops.

Summer's End

The full moon lingers
over the misty morning horizon
incongruous and dream-like.
Willow fronds fading yellow,
Canadian geese, fleeing
Above flames of autumn leaves,
warn me of winter's harshness.
Early morning sun,
sifting, diffuse,
gives soft light.
The cat leaps from shadows
to capture the brand new
wisps of sunlight.

Syntactic Analysis

Was it magic, or just magical?
Noun, solid and definite,
or only adjective, qualifying
a day in our lives?
Could it – should it – be verb,
moving us to further action?
Or can we be content,
more – can we treasure –
that which is magical,
for its own unanalyzability?

Hendaye

Lonesomeness follows
through the wind-chilled
winding
narrow streets
down to the sea
into dim candle rooms
hung with salty nets.

Between smoke nets
in weathered ageless eyes
above seafaring beards
awesome
far-blown dreams
left in memories
by the mercies
of green frothing midnight
sea thunders
are tossed
...while the mournful
wretched whine of a tomcat
chases the never-still night
breeze.

Motionless

she sat for hours
in the sun
drying her rain-cleansed body
then touched by the warmth
she raced the wind

gazelle

Hilton Head

early winter
the Carolina sun
streams through the brush
in single shafts
I pause in my morning reverie
face to face
with a soft-eyed deer
pausing, too, in her dawn excursion
by ten a.m. she and I will be dinosaurs
replaced by golfers
in bright yellow pants
who don't see the underbrush
curse the sand
and work hard at relaxing

Reassessment, on Your Being Far Away

I miss you
but we say need

do we need
or only want?

actually
one needs very little
when you get right down to it
most of this life
is really
unrecognized luxury

I need
  the stillness of the cool
  crisp morning air
  the dappling of sunlight
  through winter branches
  the warmth of my cup
  with its aromatic coffee
...and you

Out of the Study Window, Early

The bleak sun barely lights
rowhouse rooftops
and ancient chimneys.
North London shivers awake.
Pearl gray pigeons
shine pink and green,
A ray of winter's morning
reveals a rainbowed oil-slick street.

Color comes again.
We are granted one more
English winter's morn,
one more day
to look beyond the mists
and learn
the hidden hues of life.

As I Walked In the Alleys

As I walked in the alleys
the darkness spoke to me,
telling me, as it used to,
of my love affair with the world.
Tonight I listened.

Will tomorrow's icy, categorical
compartmentalization of intellectual trivia,
classifications and clocks,
fill my ears once again
with the humdrum rumblings
of scheduled living?

I Live with an Elephant

I live with an elephant
who wakes me by sitting on my chest
every morning
just about five.
He won't let me sleep
but isn't much help
at getting me out of bed,
especially on cool fall mornings.

For a while there
I thought he was gone,
but then you said good-bye
and I found him back,
having gained some weight.

I Need Some Tiny Wedges

I need some tiny wedges
to even the tilt on my bookshelves.
The longer they carry their heavy loads
the more they lean forward,
not eager
just overburdened.
A few stray pieces of wood
will solve the problem.
Simple supports, properly done
will suffice.

And for me?
What small wedges
under my toes
will even out the burdens
life has levied
as they accumulate
and I begin to lean
under their weight?

Tears Stain My Cheeks

flaming down my face
branding me with misery
how odd
that they leave no visible mark

Women Coping

Scarlet O'Hara wasn't such a silly one.
Maybe we could all learn
a lot about how to get through modern life
from her
"I don't have to think about that today,
I can think about that tomorrow."
More realistic than Annie's sun
which will come out tomorrow.
only a day away,
Scarlet puts off 'til tomorrow
what can (but need not) be done today.
Annie says it'll get better,
while Barbra Streisand
marches her band out
'cause nobody but nobody
is gonna rain on her parade.
Frankly
I think Scarlet will survive far better.
But then
I don't really have to decide today,
I can think about that tomorrow!

In the Shadow of My Honor

In the shadow of my honor
I stand immobile.
Temptation lingers, taunts.
I taste but cannot eat,
I reach but cannot touch.
Love, unreasonably, seeks to reason.
I, however, cannot.

Restarting

Shall I chase away the Monday blues
on this rainy day of March winds
by nesting, cleaning bathrooms,
scrubbing the stains from my life,
or by braving the drizzle
to trim dead twigs from the lily bed
and clear away last year's grasses,
to make room for the rebirth
I must believe is forthcoming,
promised by crocus buds?

Can I take hope that my life,
like the neat Japanese garden I nurture,
will need only a day's clearing and raking
to restore orderliness,
to surge into fresh clean beauty
and renew itself with the joy
of yet another beginning?
When do the perennials stop coming back,
when does the promise end,
and when am I too old for new beginnings?

The Pecan Grove

I. Daybreak

The trees in the grove
tall and looming
in the early morning ground fog
dwarf me.
I am a child again
and for just a moment
life is full of mystery
limited to the sphere
of that fog-bound field
yet reaching
to universes beyond.
Then the sun
burns off the mystery
revealing the interim world
that daily
I must face.

But now I know
there's something out there!

II. Midday

In the pecan grove
amid frivolous flowers
rejoicing in spring
the austere trees
bring forth shy
nearly green buds
cautious

as a new lover
vulnerable and shy
belying their stern
exterior.

I can foresee
the trees in full summer sun
tall forbidding structures
straight and stern.
Images of fathers and grandfathers,
they will flourish green and golden
producing lush leaves in Carolina sun
with the strength of a lover
showing me constancy
freeing me to laughter
to green and golden feelings
to the wanderings of
childhood innocence
blossoming, then
mellowing to full summer foliage,
anticipating the comfort
of autumn's respite
and winter's sleep.

III. Twilight

The pecan trees called to me
at day's end,
coaxing me to a magic time
when once again the grove exists.
The rest is gone,
the world is lush green
ever-deepening hues
in mystical inviting shadows.

The black cat romps,
Halloween beast dancing sideways
his bristled tail a warning
to would-be shadow foes,
then leaps, laughing in play.
Darkness has come so silently
that I didn’t hear
its fear,
only felt its softness.

Gray Morning Rain

Gray morning rain
and the angry wind
mirror my pain
and the emptiness you have left
in your going.

I hear the wind at my door,
shut out, as you have now shut me out.
We said so many things
in our practical discussion
of how to proceed in a relationship
in which we are afraid
of hurt and loss.

Did we let our fears
outstrip the love we feel,
the happiness we had finally found
in each other?

What in particular did I say
that finally pierced your defenses,
causing such anguish
that barriers went up,
that I can no longer reach you,
that I am once again alone
wondering why
once again I have failed.

Funeral at St. Sulpice

Someone is dead
while spring
vaguely struggles
to emerge
amidst the Paris ordure.
A little boy urinates
in a corner
next to a flower vendor's wagon
in the Latin Quarter.
A beggar steals bread
from pigeons more loved than he.
Passing in the street,
the black, well polished
around clean glass
clashes with pinks and oranges
in its windows,
tulips breathing the nausea
of misery
that someone has escaped.

Pop

The top of my clear glass pumpkin jar
broke today.
It had a stem for a handle,
and was just like a jack-o-lantern top,
but the glass pumpkin had no Halloween face.
It was just a pumpkin,
the one that Pop used to keep
raspberry candies in,
the kind with soft centers
tart but sweet
gooey with syrup on the inside
but hard on the outside
like Pop,
tough and weathered.
He stirred his coffee with his thumb
and smoked strong offensive-smelling
nickel stogies,
but he always had raspberry candies
(a sweet tooth, my father called it)
and he always had time for us.

On cold winter mornings
we descended in the oil-soaked gas station
to the dark, low-ceilinged cellar
where the big smokey coal furnace burned,
with a loaf of raisin bread.
Pop would show us, always teaching the same lesson,
how to gently lay aside the icing from each slice
then weave the bread onto a long old fork
and toast its cinnamon spirals
over the white hot coals --
Don't get too close --

then replace the icing strips
and spread homemade apple butter
on the warm crusty bread.
My brother and I would share the treat
with Pop.

As we grew older
the baker quit delivering
and Pop started wintering in Florida,
so we didn't go down in the cellar anymore.
And they quit making those raspberry candies,
and Grandma took the glass pumpkin home
and filled it with bills on the kitchen cupboard.
Pop still stirred his coffee with his thumb
but it wasn't the same.

One night I woke
in our house up on the hill
overlooking Pop's gas station
and heard my parents' voices.
In pajamas I walked into the shivery winter night
to see the light
and stand by my brother in awe
as the oil-soaked cellar
and the special office
where the pumpkin jar used to sit
and the gas pumps and the stools we sat on
all burned
in a magnificent blaze
that Pop wasn't there to see.
He had taken Grandma to Florida
to get away from the cold.
I wished he could see.
My dad said it would only make him sad
but I knew he would have wanted to say good-bye

to the memories of raspberry candies
and raisin bread winters with icing and apple butter
and summertime sodas.
I cried for Pop,
and my brother said don't be a dumb girl.

I moved far away
to another state and another world
of books and professors and students,
foreign to Pop.

One night at supper in Florida
he dropped his glass of water,
spilled it all over himself,
and Grandma yelled at him.
He couldn't answer, and when he vomited
my father cleaned him up and called me.
"I think he had a stroke, but it's over now.
He can't talk though.
He needs to go home to Pennsylvania,"
my father told me on the phone.
My father understood
that Pop needed to be near the land
where the old oil-soaked gas station had stood,
to be with the memories,
to smell the raisin bread toast
and taste the raspberry candies
with my brother and me
one more time,
in that private world he had now entered,
before he left us.

Now the pumpkin jar
sits on my kitchen counter
full of tea.

Last night something fell,
just like Pop's water glass,
and the top broke
diminishing my ability
to summon the memories
that break up now, like glass,
more fragile with increasing age.

Grandma's Gone

Grandma's gone now.
She died last night
bringing our own mortality
to the forefront
of awareness.
Her peace has come at last
leaving us with sadness,
the memories of poignant early days
and the bittersweet sense
of having kept her too long
when she longed to go.
Ninety-seven years,
a decade or more
beyond her peers.
Loneliness is being the last to go
Mercifully for her,
she was not the last…
for we are here.

Kites

brilliantly colored, red yellow green
they dance against the gray coastal sky
beach houses, weathered to match the storms
boldly stand watch over vacant beaches
distant rumbling thunder warns
as crackling, jagged threads of light
unravel against the sky
and are gone like spirits
almost imperceptibly
soft drops of rain splash on the sand
wet the kites
caress the earth
it's time to reel in our late afternoon
fold it up
and take it indoors

Good-bye

hope leaps
golden
mirrored in eyes
semi-dies
to a red amber spot
gray flecks
of future memories
fall to the floor
and acquaintance
is ended
in an ashtray

Picking Berries

Home to visit parents
for the 4th of July,
I walk carefully in my city clothes
behind my father
in the wild raspberry patches
armed with Mother's plastic containers.
He steps down the brambles
and leaves large choice clusters for me.
I remember,
pick only the shiny black ones
that aren't yet dull
and overripe.
They must readily fall into the bowl;
if they cling to the stem
they aren't ready.
"Can't believe the birds didn't find these,"
he marvels, absorbed in the task.
I delight in the colors --
pale green ghostly ones on the outside of each cluster
then red ones
and in the center
shiny round bursting black
sugary and full, tempting me.
My bowl full, I pick on,
eating every third one,
piling the rest on top.
Dad breaks trail along the woods' edge
leading me now
as I led him years ago.
"There are probably some by the fallen walnut tree."
He knows where the best patches are.
He never used to know.

I knew, and when he could spare the time
on a weekend I would show him.
Now the territory is his,
and the task of finding time, mine.
Tired, hot and sticky
we bring our booty to Mother's kitchen.
She cleans berries and praises us,
just as she used to.
My purple fingers are
for a moment
those of a tired little girl
who has eaten her fill of raspberries
spending a Pennsylvania Saturday afternoon
picking berries with Daddy.
Those times will never come again.
But neither will these.

Accident

death

Our love was purple, idyllic beauty
Inconceivable for any end but violence.
Our innocence was shattered in
royal death, a lightening-sped purging
of thick slow red
spilling over mangled glinting steel.
A purple crimson flood
drained graying flesh,
yet was known only as a telegram's
colorless sparks,
static sounds of potential horror realized,
leaving indigo thoughts.

grief

In the purple storms of pain,
crimson rage, the masochistic drive
to sheer exhaustion
of body temple-prisons
darkens, bloodlets to blue
and grays.

Despair, a prison of broken prisms
and colorless rainbows,
is a fetus of the mind
too dead to bleed.

beyond

I am alone.
Madness
beast that haunts the night
crawling slyly in ears
to gnaw at sleeping brains
where minds were once,
grotesque horror, a beast
that feasts, insatiable
leaves a tormented soul
for the mind he eats.

recovery

Yesterday and life
incomplete the spectrum
in which tomorrow lacks.
Indigo, faded by still sun
and pulsing rain,
adds ever-changing hues.
Faded blues sustain.
I shall go on.

Ode to My Dead Sister

Daydreaming
as I sat at my desk
the trumpet music held me
though I wasn't aware of why
until I saw you
silver trumpet gleaming
like your golden hair
cascading in curls
and swirls of sound.

Memories of my nearly grown
little sister
    lifting me out of myself
    with lyric notes
    I both savored and envied
strike a sad chord.

In the defined frame
of my office window
a group of blackbirds
lift in unison
move in concert to a tall barren tree.
take their places unhesitatingly
    notes returning to sheet music,
    a silent melody
    in the cold winter sun,
then depart
as the sad trumpet strains fade.

Sister
you have gone
taken your music,
left a sweet sadness
as I grow old without you.

Death is a Woman

I have felt her cold breath on my cheek
over my shoulder, as she jealously steals those I love,
as she entices me when at my most vulnerable.
She has shown me her methods:
her slow insidious side, cancerous,
tumor-like, gnawing life away;
her flashing anger of grinding steel and breaking glass;
the stealth of softly purring carbon-monoxide sleep,
one's own hand doing her work;
and the evil of another's hand
secretly offering a lethal dose,
retribution for sins of noncompliance.
She, who has shown me each to frighten and impress,
now coaxes, enticing with an exit and a promise,
having taught me her craft.
Shall I test my apprenticeship?

Nuclear

is he talking about family
or a weapon of destruction?
Perhaps, for him
they are one

Battling Ghosts

Your ghosts are bigger than my ghosts
Your ghosts are bigger than mine
Your ghosts are stronger than my ghosts
Your ghosts are becoming mine

I wish I knew more of your ghosts
You need know little of mine
I wish I knew more of your ghosts
They alter my keen sense of time

My ghosts are shrinking, not your ghosts
My ghosts are ready to fall
My ghosts now haunt very little
Yet your ghosts still cast a pall

Your ghosts aren't fading like my ghosts
My ghosts are shrinking in the past
Your ghosts still hold you quite firmly
How long will their haunting last?

How can we rid us of your ghosts
How can we finally be free
I can't do battle with your ghosts
They started so long before me

How long can we live with your ghosts
Before our love will succumb?
How can we exorcize your ghosts
And move to new conundrums?

Friday Street

A drop of dew
Hangs fragile on the moss
Capturing a glint of sun
It takes in light
Gleams radiantly
Seducing

Seeking a deeper experience
I touch it
My finger wets, too late
It's gone

I am alone
In the deep emerald ferns
Under the forest canopy
And the sun's light
Now has no messenger
To light my way

Endings

Jeanne is dead.
A rude shock, the unreality of it
clutches at me.
White sycamore trunks
skeletal against darker winter trees
gleam in the late afternoon sun.
A whisper of white moon
eerie shadow in the daylight
solidifies with the coming grayness of dusk.
The headlights of oncoming cars
flicker through the median guard rail
as we drive home from the funeral,
across the desolate winter landscape.

The indelible picture
is locked in my mind
of a stained pine coffin
and twelve long-stemmed red roses…
Laura Beth, only fifteen,
the freshness of her youth
turned gray with grief…
Her mother's left her standing there
in black
holding two red roses.
Silently she drops one
into the grave
and turns away.

Stillbirth

a single semi-solid sound
writhing across a liquid gray
skew-lined chamber
tilts
till a shriek
tears the semi-solid
clotted silence, dead, dry
and smothers
even the sibilant blood flow
birth sounds echo in my soul
never to be heard
pain draws me off
to eerie dreams
I cry within

Mirror Image

My mirror image sees me
Am I awake
as we turn
and I see you next to me
watching?

I reach toward your image
and see my reaching clearly
mirrored in the shining glass
but turning, find you gone.

Sister, you have gone.
Are you still by my side
guiding, prodding?
Have you left this shade
more me than you
yet a transparency
to help me find the essence of you
that hovers
just beyond my consciousness?

Competition no longer,
are you critic and conscience now?
In death you have not grown
larger than life
but linger
just the other side of the mirror.

As the aroma of morning coffee
teases me back
the shadow of she
whom you left me
steps through the glimmer
of my mirror.

Will you return?
Are you she, or part me?
And how will I know?
The knowingness recedes
to just beyond the window
and I can feel but not quite see
that tangible
intangible wisp of sensation
slipping away.

I am me
but not only
and not quite whole
I am you
but not entirely.
We are becoming,
and I alone yet with you
must be the one,
looking back and looking out,
to complete the cycle.

Recovery

My love says he has no future.
His present, however, is sometimes with me,
and I would like a future.

The future is what keeps me going
I tell him,
the music soft in the background.

That's very reasonable,
he says, yet it's clear
that it strikes him as a new idea.

Who has done such damage
to her fellow man
as to leave him
without a future
that I could be part of,
to shut him so far away
that while he loves me
he cannot accept, reach out,
need, want, express.

How long do I wait?
And what are the signs
of repair that might open his life
to sharing?
If I choose not to wait,
how then do I stop loving
this enigma who has no future?

The Crab

The fiddler crab
cautiously peeks from a hole in the sand
then darts back.
Is he playing with me, or truly frightened?
As he reveals himself, a miracle of nature,
miniaturized, yet perfect in every detail,
I realize my insignificance.
I am no being to elicit his play
or engender fear,
but a large blur of movement
signaling possible danger,
only some large change in light
to be avoided in enhancing survival,
otherwise unthought of.
And this marvelous miniature
cares not a grain of sand
what I think of him.
Only we humans have an ego so great
as to believe that all creatures
consider us
in their view of the world.

Saturday Morning

fog shrouds my little house
on the Japanese cherry tree
the buds are swollen
the air is warm
enticing me outdoors
and for a brief moment
I am isolated
surrounded by a safe little world
with no one crying
and no one dying
just the peace of me, alone
and a single early daffodil

Shore Ghosts

early morning footprints
in the sand

deeper in the toe
he was running
    an early morning jaunt
    or an urgent return
    to some sleeping lover

toes grasping individually, small foot
she greeted the morning sand barefoot, quickly
    communing with earth
    glorying in the sun
    and the deserted morning

big dog, small dog
    together? no
    one is deeper, running
    keeping pace with his master
    one shallow, full prints,
    meandering
    with his elderly charges

shoes on the surface
a couple
    strolling
    savoring the quiet
    joining with the rushing surf sounds
    unhurried

yet I am here alone
with my own ghosts
no one in sight
on the vast sands

Mating Rituals

a lone bird
on the single roof peak
chirps monotonously, then stops

I sit alone
in the single deck chair
gazing at the horizon
lost in thought of no thought

he screeches in short bursts
and with clear release
launches into song
trilling and chirping pure melody

my pulse quickens
my spirits rise
perhaps I will stroll to the beach
mingle with the crowd
of summer vacationers
tanned and enticing

a pause
and he couples his song
with a brief flight
straight up from the peak
then dips, flutters up again
and in fluttering, hovers
    oh look at me
    please look
    I am so grand
    come join me
then settles

dejected and alone
to the roof peak
resuming his single tones

fatigue overcomes me
it's too far to walk
the beach
over the dunes I sit watching
full of strangers
intent on their own
holiday preoccupations

but soon
this tiny bird will leap
his hope renewed
and he will replay
his optimistic musical repertoire
opening once again
his search for a mate

the bird is far less prone
to becoming a lonely recluse
will nature's urges
protect me
as they do him?

Afternoon Nap on the Porch

Sleep calls me away
from thoughts of you
gently, tenderly,
only to tease me awake with dreams.
I feel the rain caressing my face,
hear the wind carrying night jasmine scents
to awaken my heart
though my body would sleep.
And when I see you,
where shall we go?

We Talked Through the Night

the rain and the mercury light
on the lifeless pavement outside
made patterns
shadow sounds
not unlike our being
when the rain ceased
leaving
the haze of dreamless unreality
we slept
awake and dreamlike
was the cool automatic
mercury light

Sailboats

sailboats dazzle, white
like the bleached
starched collars
of little boys' sailor suits
or freshly polished
high-top leather shoes

the breeze
carrying them smoothly
evenly
across my line of vision
across the bay
also carries away
the last of summer

radios mingling
with gull cries
sandy novels
and the sweet smell of tanning oil
give way to crisp cool mornings
misted car windows
dew on the grass
yellow school buses clogging traffic
and styles of darker colors
foreshadowing the changing foliage

the world will again turn serious
and pristine white sails
like frivolous ruffles
on little girls' dresses
will greedily envelope the wind
our sole reminders of summer

Finding My Lost Sister

I.
I was Daddy's tomboy
whom he wanted to name
for his bomber squadron buddy.
He let me climb trees,
took me to work on car engines,
praised me for getting dirty,
running fast,
and climbing trees.

But then the little blonde-haired baby came
An angel, feminine and pretty.
I taught her to run,
get dirty, be irreverent,
to no avail.
A gymnast, she still
had long blonde hair
and beauty with which I was not blessed,
and I was still the tomboy
with short dark unruly hair
and good grades,
overachieving to win love
and acceptance.

She tried to give me all of that
by making me the "only daughter,"
leaving early
in a storm,
drowning herself and our dreams for her
in one quick moment,
slipping into the turmoil
of a hurricane's rushing death,

snuffing the light in her hair and eyes
that spoke of exciting futures.

But they still call me
"our oldest daughter."
She hasn't left us entirely
and often I long for
the sister I was learning to love
and the one I was learning to be.
Both are gone now.

II.
We kept our girlhood treasures,
secrets in velvet-lined boxes.
Miniature caskets, I called them,
hers pink, mine blue.
Hers contained pretty stones,
then flowers, and wilted corsages,
mine insect cases, cocoons.
The beauty is inside, I said,
someday you'll understand.

One year she gave me a box just for me,
no other like it,
lovingly crafted as my surprise,
white ceramic with rosebuds, pink and delicate;
when she said it was like me
I laughed.

III.
I have guarded my grief
for the two of us
in an inlaid box of precious woods
and pearlized shells
like the treasures we once collected,
walking forests and beaches.

I take it out, this grief,
examine it gently,
sense the healing of each memory
worn and comfortable now,
caress its rounded corners
and almost can't recall
sharp edges that used to cut.

From the box
come echoes of childhood laughter.
They call me forth
as dulled pain pushes
from behind,
forcing me out of my chrysalis
into the warm sunshine,
feeling safe as I dry my wings
flex them
and, taking all that she left me,
all that I have treasured of the two of us,
realize that I am one
able to stretch and fly
ready to look, finally
at the intricacy of design and color
of the wings of love she gave me.

Pap-pap's Garden

Pap-pap's garden was always full of color
red and yellow and purple columbines
delicate as angels in the summer sun.

Every week he brought the eggs
in his old tan Plymouth
smelling of cigarettes and Old Spice.

And every week in spring and summer
a bouquet of flowers would come along,
an eagerly anticipated surprise.

The garden is grown over with weeds
and the house sits empty.
As I walk the narrow cement path,
uneven now, with moss in the cracks,
I find a columbine gone to seed.
Ugly and brown, fat to bursting,
it holds a secret bouquet
of colorful Sunday memories
which I shall plant,
and patiently wait
for a bouquet
from my grandfather's garden.

Distance

My husband
Alone, so far away
Do you always love me?
Or do you forget
Preoccupied with tasks
Energized to deal with emergencies
Focused for the moment
On the lives and deaths of others?

I know when the storm is ended
That you think of me
Would recount your day
Share your triumphs, humbly,
Voice your cares, tersely,
But am I in your heart
Under the layers
Deep in your being
As you are in mine?

Going Home for Christmas, Together

Wind-drifted snow
obscured the road
as we shopped for Amish quilts
and antique treasures
in valleys created by tired old
central Pennsylvania mountains.
Shocks of cornstalks
on snowy fields,
horses and buggies in somber colors,
ruddy German-American complexions,
mingled with our footprints
in the new powdery snow.
Snowflakes drifting gently
outside the multitude of window panes,
shared moments --
unshared memories --
contribute to who we are
and to our mutual delight
in one another.

Home

in the fine mist of rain
I lovingly planted
all the wildflowers
from the Pennsylvania farm
my bit of country
brought home
a respite for eye
and soul
from the city's driving tempo

soil under fingernails
nourishing my roots
replenished by occasional visits
sustains

Promise

in the cool gray morning
of almost winter
lingering birds
dive into branches
of barren trees
in a colorless world

my mind sees colors
from warm spring rain
of crocus, budding snowdrops
and your kaleidoscopic eyes
there is hope
in waiting

As I Approach Four Score and Four

as I approach
four score and four
taking life
and asking more
the sunshine warms my soul

After Forty

The philosopher said that after forty
all of life is spiritual.
TS Eliot has measured life
in coffee spoons, trying to decide
about eating peaches and walking on beaches.
Much more poetic than today
when dying my hair or going gray,
giving in to bifocals, or squinting a while yet,
and what to microwave for dinner
are my preoccupations.
Well, Mr. Philosopher, is it still true?
Eyes are the windows of soul,
so maybe when the squint takes more effort
and the cataracts cloud
it's time to look inward and upward,
to walk on the beach without seeing.
And maybe the philosopher was right.

Printed in the United States
17844LVS00005B/59